Number Rhymes

One horse

Reproducible emergent readers
to make and take home

By Jean Warren

Illustrated by Kelly McMahon and Cora Walker-Carleson

Totline® Publications
A Division of Frank Schaffer Publications, Inc.
Torrance, California

Managing Editor: Mina McMullin
Contributing Editors: Gayle Bittinger, Jean Warren
Copyeditor: Kathy Zaun
Editorial Assistant: Mary Newmaster
Graphic Designer (Interior): Jill Kaufman
Graphic Designer (Cover): Brenda Mann Harrison
Production Manager: Janie Schmidt

Parts of this book have been previously published by Totline® Publications as Totline® "Take-Home" Books— Alphabet and Number Rhymes.

ISBN: 1-57029-301-5

Printed in the United States of America
Published by Totline® Publications
23740 Hawthorne Blvd.
Torrance, CA 90505

Contents

(The page numbers listed above are on the inside margins of each page.)

Introduction

Young children love books and want so badly to be able to read them. Many times, you can see young children holding books and using the pictures to "read" them. Totline Reproducible Rhyme Books are the perfect way to help young children experience the thrill of "reading" as they also learn other valuable concepts.

Each of the ten beginning emergent readers in *Number Rhymes* contains exciting illustrations which enable young children to "read" them. In addition, these books feature beginning number concepts important for all children to learn. Children can practice adding, subtracting, and other math skills.

All of the books in this series are reproducible, so each child can have his or her own copy. Directions for using the books and ideas for decorating covers for them and for extending the learning are provided on page 4.

You will love watching your children glow with pride and experience such feelings of success when they take home their very own books to "read" to their families.

Assembly and Directions for Use

1. Tear out the pages for the book of your choice.

2. For double-sided copies, copy the pages exactly as they are and then cut the pages in half. For single-sided pages, simply copy the pages for each child and cut them in half.

3. Give each child two 5½-by-8-inch pieces of construction paper to use for book covers. Let the children decorate their covers as desired or use one of the suggestions listed below. (See Cover Decorating Ideas.)

4. If desired, place the book pages on a table and let the children help collate them into books. (Younger children may need help with this process.)

5. Help the children bind their books using a stapler or a hole punch and paper fasteners.

6. Before letting the children work on their books, go over them page by page.

7. Point out the featured numbers and any words you feel the children should pay particular attention to.

8. As some stories require the children to fill in particular numbers for answers, be sure to discuss these. Make certain the children know how to write these numbers and assist any children who might need help.

Cover Decorating Ideas

1. Let the children use rubber stamps to print objects that correspond to the book's subject on their covers.

2. Make paint pads by folding paper towels, placing them in shallow containers, and pouring small amounts of tempera paint on them. Then give the children cookie cutters or sponges cut in the appropriate shapes. Have them dip their cookie cutters or sponges into the paint and then press them on their covers.

3. Let the children cut out and glue magazine pictures on their covers.

4. Have the children write their names on the back covers of their books.

5. Older children can write "This book belongs to _____" on their back covers.

6. Let older children draw objects of their choice on their covers and write each object's name next to it.

Extended Learning Ideas

1. Enlarge the pages of a book to make a big book. Let the children color the illustrations on the pages.

2. Incorporate the books into a larger theme unit.

3. Let your children find and color the main object in a story. Then have them color the rest of the pictures.

4. To help the children learn more or different numbers, add pages to their books. You can write a simple verse and let the children draw pictures and trace or write numbers.

5. Let older children copy a rhyme onto other sheets of paper and illustrate.

6. Older children can practice writing any featured numbers or words you choose from a particular rhyme.

7. Older children can add extra pages to their books. Let them continue writing a rhyme on their own or in groups. Or, let them create a new rhyme using new numbers.

5

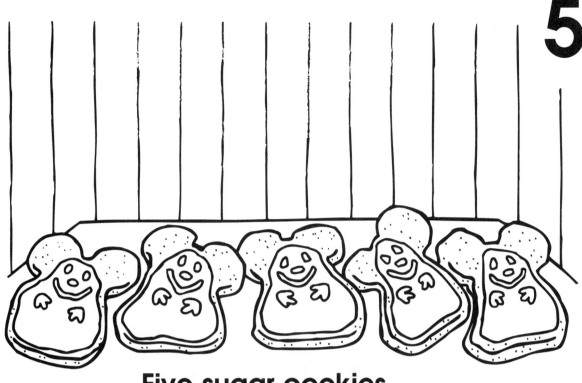

**Five sugar cookies
With frosting galore**

1

4

**Four sugar cookies
Two and two, you see.**

3

Mother ate one.

Then there were _____.

p 6 © 2001 Totline® Publications

Father ate one.

Then there were _____.

p 6 © 2001 Totline® Publications

3

**Three sugar cookies,
And before I knew**

5

2

**Two sugar cookies
Oh, what fun!**

7

p 8 © 2001 Totline® Publications

Sister ate one.

6

Then there were _____.

---

p 8 © 2001 Totline® Publications

Brother ate one.

8

Then there was _____.

**One sugar cookie—
Watch me run.**

**I ate it.
Then there were none!**

10

One horse who lived on the farm

1

Two cows who lived on the farm

3

2   **Went to bed in the big old barn.**

4   **Went to bed in the big old barn.**

3

Three sheep who lived on the farm   5

4

Four goats who lived on the farm   7

6   **Went to bed in the big old barn.**

p 14 © 2001 Totline® Publications

8   **Went to bed in the big old barn.**

p 14 © 2001 Totline® Publications

5

Five pigs who lived on the farm

p 15 © 2001 Totline® Publications

6

Six rabbits who lived on the farm

p 15 © 2001 Totline® Publications

p 16 © 2001 Totline® Publications

10   **Went to bed in the big old barn.**

p 16 © 2001 Totline® Publications

12   **Went to bed in the big old barn.**

Seven ducks who lived on the farm 13

Eight dogs who lived on the farm 15

p 18 © 2001 Totline® Publications

14 **Went to bed in the big old barn.**

p 18 © 2001 Totline® Publications

16 **Went to bed in the big old barn.**

9

Nine cats who lived on the farm 17

10

Ten chicks who lived on the farm 19

p 20 © 2001 Totline® Publications

18 **Went to bed in the big old barn.**

p 20 © 2001 Totline® Publications

20 **Went to bed in the big old barn.**

Shhh!

21

On the first day of summer,
What did I see?

1

On the second day of summer,
What did I see?

3

A robin up in a tree

p 24 © 2001 Totline® Publications

2

**Two ducks swimming
And a robin up in a tree**

p 24 © 2001 Totline® Publications

4

On the third day of summer,
What did I see?

On the fourth day of summer,
What did I see?

**Three bees buzzing,
Two ducks swimming,
And a robin up in a tree**

6

**Four dogs barking, three bees buzzing,
Two ducks swimming,
And a robin up in a tree**

8

p 27 © 2001 Totline® Publications

**On the fifth day of summer,
What did I see?**

p 27 © 2001 Totline® Publications

**On the sixth day of summer,
What did I see?**

Five picnic baskets, four dogs barking,
Three bees buzzing,
Two ducks swimming,
And a robin up in a tree

10

p 28 © 2001 Totline® Publications

Six flowers growing, five picnic baskets,
Four dogs barking, three bees buzzing,
Two ducks swimming,
And a robin up in a tree

12

p 28 © 2001 Totline® Publications

10

Ten little bunnies jumping on the bed, 1

9

Nine little bunnies jumping on the bed, 3

**One fell off and bumped her head.
How many bunnies
Jumping on the bed?_____**

p 30 © 2001 Totline® Publications

**One fell off and bumped his head.
How many bunnies
Jumping on the bed?_____**

p 30 © 2001 Totline® Publications

Eight little bunnies jumping on the bed, 5

Seven little bunnies jumping on the bed, 7

**One fell off and bumped her head.
How many bunnies
Jumping on the bed?**_____

p 32 © 2001 Totline® Publications

**One fell off and bumped his head.
How many bunnies
Jumping on the bed?**_____

p 32 © 2001 Totline® Publications

Six little bunnies jumping on the bed, 9

Five little bunnies jumping on the bed, 11

p 34 © 2001 Totline® Publications

One fell off and bumped her head.
How many bunnies
Jumping on the bed?_____

10

p 34 © 2001 Totline® Publications

One fell off and bumped his head.
How many bunnies
Jumping on the bed?_____

12

4

Four little bunnies jumping on the bed, 13

3

Three little bunnies jumping on the bed, 15

p 36 © 2001 Totline® Publications

One fell off and bumped her head.
How many bunnies
14 **Jumping on the bed?_____**

p 36 © 2001 Totline® Publications

One fell off and bumped his head.
How many bunnies
16 **Jumping on the bed?_____**

2

Two little bunnies jumping on the bed,   17

1

One little bunny jumping on the bed,   19

One fell off and bumped her head.
How many bunnies
Jumping on the bed?_____

p 38 © 2001 Totline® Publications

18

He fell off and bumped his head.
How many bunnies
Jumping on the bed?_____

p 38 © 2001 Totline® Publications

20

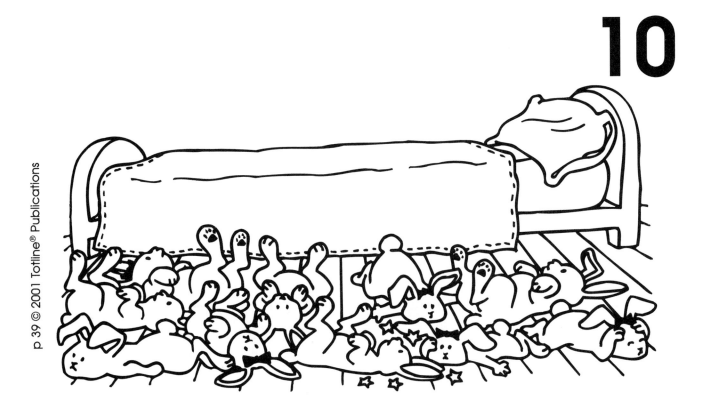

Ten little bunnies lying on the floor   21

22 "Get back to bed and jump no more!"

p 40 © 2001 Totline® Publications

1

**One little bug went out to play
On a spider's web one day.**

1

2

**Two little bugs went out to play
On a spider's web one day.**

3

p 42 © 2001 Totline® Publications

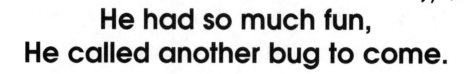

**He had so much fun,
He called another bug to come.**

2

p 42 © 2001 Totline® Publications

**They had so much fun,
They called another bug to come.**

4

3

**Three little bugs went out to play
On a spider's web one day.**

5

4

**Four little bugs went out to play
On a spider's web one day.**

7

p 44 © 2001 Totline® Publications

**They had so much fun,
They called another bug to come.**

6

p 44 © 2001 Totline® Publications

**They had so much fun,
They called another bug to come.**

8

5

**Five little bugs went out to play
On a spider's web one day.**

9

p 46 © 2001 Totline® Publications

They got stuck in a bunch.
Along came a spider in time for lunch!

10

10

Ten little crabs who lived in the sea　　1

9

Nine little fish who lived in the sea　　3

p 48 © 2001 Totline® Publications

**Jumped in the boat
With Skipper and me.**

2

p 48 © 2001 Totline® Publications

**Jumped in the boat
With Skipper and me.**

4

8

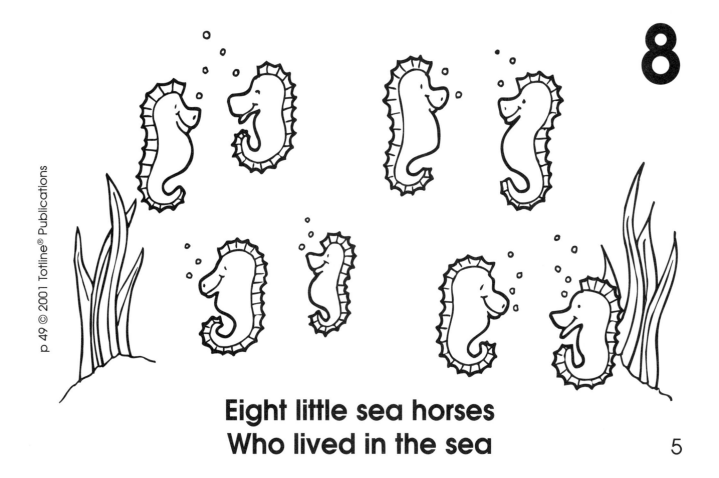

**Eight little sea horses
Who lived in the sea**

5

7

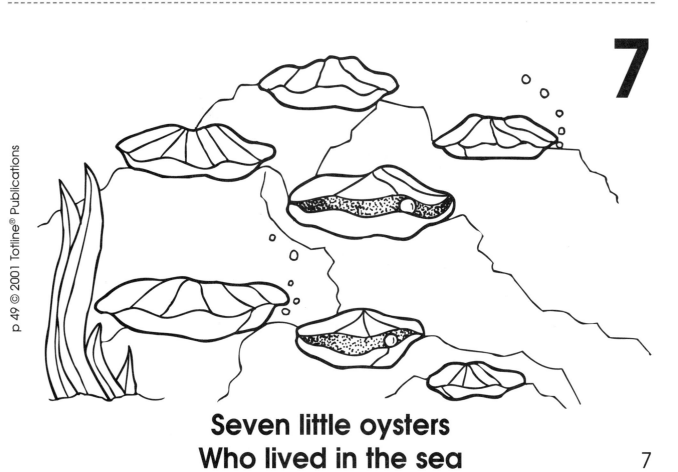

**Seven little oysters
Who lived in the sea**

7

Jumped in the boat
With Skipper and me.

p 50 © 2001 Totline® Publications

Jumped in the boat
With Skipper and me.

p 50 © 2001 Totline® Publications

6

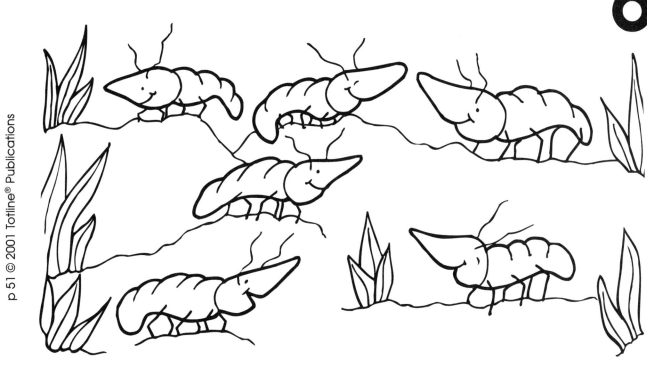

Six little shrimp who lived in the sea 9

5

Five little sea stars who lived in the sea 11

**Jumped in the boat
With Skipper and me.**

10

p 52 © 2001 Totline® Publications

12

**Jumped in the boat
With Skipper and me.**

p 52 © 2001 Totline® Publications

4

Four little octopuses
Who lived in the sea

13

3

Three little sharks
Who lived in the sea

15

**Jumped in the boat
With Skipper and me.**

14

p 54 © 2001 Totline® Publications

**Jumped in the boat
With Skipper and me.**

16

p 54 © 2001 Totline® Publications

2

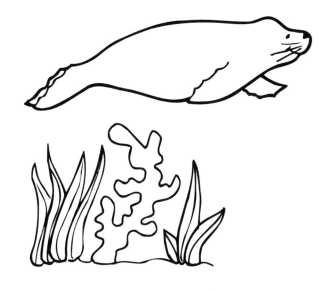

Two little seals who lived in the sea   17

- -

1

One little whale who lived in the sea   19

**Jumped in the boat
With Skipper and me.**

18

p 56 © 2001 Totline® Publications

**Jumped in the boat
With Skipper and me.**

20

p 56 © 2001 Totline® Publications

**How many boots should the little duck buy
To keep his feet nice and dry?_____**

1

**How many boots should the little cat buy
To keep her feet nice and dry?_____**

3

2

**Two little boots is what he should buy
To keep his feet nice and dry.**

2

p 58 © 2001 Totline® Publications

4

**Four little boots is what she should buy
To keep her feet nice and dry.**

4

p 58 © 2001 Totline® Publications

p 59 © 2001 Totline® Publications

**How many boots should the little ant buy
To keep his feet nice and dry?_____**

5

p 59 © 2001 Totline® Publications

**How many boots should the little pig buy
To keep her feet nice and dry?_____**

7

6

**Six little boots is what he should buy
To keep his feet nice and dry.**

p 60 © 2001 Totline® Publications

6

4

**Four little boots is what she should buy
To keep her feet nice and dry.**

p 60 © 2001 Totline® Publications

8

**How many boots should the little crab buy
To keep his feet nice and dry?_____**   9

**How many boots should the little fish buy
To keep her feet nice and dry?_____**   11

8

**Eight little boots is what he should buy
To keep his feet nice and dry.**

10

0

**Zero little boots is what she should buy
To keep her feet nice and dry.**

12

Five little cookies by the door

1

Four little cookies by the tree

3

Mother ate one.
Now there are four.

Father ate one.
Now there are three.

Three little cookies by the shoe

5

Two little cookies just got done.

7

Sister ate one.
Now there are two.

p 66 © 2001 Totline® Publications

Brother ate one.
Now there is one.

p 66 © 2001 Totline® Publications

One little cookie, the only one

9

p 68 © 2001 Totline® Publications

I ate it.
Now there are none.

10

10

Ten little bears riding on the train
Looks like it is going to rain.

1

8

Eight little bears riding on the train
Looks like it is going to rain.

3

p 70 © 2001 Totline® Publications

**Two little bears get off the train.
How many bears are now
Riding on the train?____**

2

- -

p 70 © 2001 Totline® Publications

**Two more bears get off the train.
How many bears are now
Riding on the train?____**

4

**Six little bears riding on the train
Looks like it is going to rain.**

p 71 © 2001 Totline® Publications

**Four little bears riding on the train
Looks like it is going to rain.**

p 71 © 2001 Totline® Publications

p 72 © 2001 Totline® Publications

Two more bears get off the train.
How many bears are now
Riding on the train?_____

6

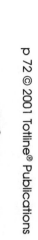

p 72 © 2001 Totline® Publications

Two more bears get off the train.
How many bears are now
Riding on the train?_____

8

2

Two little bears riding on the train
Looks like it is going to rain.

9

0

Zero bears riding on the train
Crash! Boom! Down comes the rain!

11

p 73 © 2001 Totline® Publications

p 74 © 2001 Totline® Publications

Two more bears get off the train.
How many bears are now
Riding on the train?_____

10

1

One little girl rowing in the pond 1

2

Two little birds flying over the pond 3

**Another girl comes along.
How many girls are now
Rowing in the pond?_____**

p 76 © 2001 Totline® Publications

**Two more birds come along.
How many birds are now
Flying over the pond?_____**

p 76 © 2001 Totline® Publications

3

Three little fish swimming in the pond   5

4

Four little ducks swimming in the pond   7

Another fish comes along.
How many fish are now
Swimming in the pond?_____

p 78 © 2001 Totline® Publications

Two more ducks come along.
How many ducks are now
Swimming in the pond?_____

p 78 © 2001 Totline® Publications

Five little butterflies flying over the pond

9

p 80 © 2001 Totline® Publications

Three more butterflies come along.
How many butterflies are now
Flying over the pond?_____

10